Gold Mines
and
Law Books

[Seated portrait of Hubert Howe Bancroft].

Image courtesy of California Faces: Selections from The Bancroft Library Portrait Collection, The Bancroft Library, University of California, Berkeley.

Gold Mines
and
Law Books

H. H. Bancroft's
California Bookshop

M.H. HOEFLICH &
JOHN MORELAND

TALBOT
PUBLISHING
Clark, New Jersey
2024

ISBN 978-1-61619-696-7

Interior front cover:
P1960-73-30. "Thunder Mountain Lawyers - Hawley & Puckett Office". Idaho State Archives.

Interior rear cover:
[Passenger train in mountains]. Detroit Publishing Company Photograph Collection, Prints and Photographs Division of the Library of Congress, Washington, DC.

Beard, Frank, "Does not such a meeting make amends?" Illus. in: *Frank Leslie's Illustrated Newspaper*, v. 28, no. 713 (May 29, 1869), p. 176. Prints and Photographs Division of the Library of Congress, Washington, DC.

Talbot Publishing

AN IMPRINT OF

The Lawbook Exchange, Ltd.

33 Terminal Avenue
Clark, New Jersey 07066-1321

Please see our website for a selection of our other publications and fine facsimile reprints of classic works of legal history:
www.lawbookexchange.com

Library of Congress Cataloging-in-Publication Data

Names: Hoeflich, Michael H., author. | Moreland, John (John L.), author.
Title: Gold mines and law books : H.H. Bancroft's California bookshop / M.H. Hoeflich & John Moreland.
Description: Clark, New Jersey : Talbot Publishing 2024. | Includes bibliographical references. | Summary: "This chapbook takes the reader back to Gold Rush California and evokes the triumphs of H.H. Bancroft, one of the great entrepreneurial booksellers of antebellum America"-- Provided by publisher.
Identifiers: LCCN 2024060506 | ISBN 9781616196967 (paperback ; acid-free paper)
Subjects: LCSH: Legal literature--Publishing--California--History--19th century. | Bancroft, Hubert Howe, 1832-1918. | Booksellers and bookselling--California--History--19th century.
Classification: LCC Z480.L44 H63 2024 | DDC 381/.450020979461--dc23/eng/20250208
LC record available at https://lccn.loc.gov/2024060506

Printed in the United States of America on acid-free paper

For Greg Talbot, bookseller, book publisher, and scholar.

M.H. HOEFLICH

To Doug Lind, who first showed me the world of rare books. They are indeed worth their weight in gold.

JOHN MORELAND

V ERY LITTLE has been written about law bookselling in early California.[1] Before the Gold Rush of 1849, California was a remote region, largely isolated from the rest of the antebellum United States. Travel from the Eastern states to California was long and perilous and required either a month's long overland trip across mountains and plains or a long sea voyage around Cape Horn. But after the discovery of gold at Sutter's Mill, thousands of men and women undertook the voyage in the hopes of finding wealth. As the population of California increased, commerce increased as well, accompanied by debt collection, land title disputes, and crime. Along with the merchants came bankers and lawyers. And lawyers, even in remote places, needed law books. But California was a continent away from the law book publishing and bookselling centers of New York, Philadelphia, Boston, Richmond, and Baltimore. How would California's burgeoning business community deal with the inflow of inevitable legal disputes, and by extension, the dearth of law books required by lawyers for the resolution of those disputes?

---

1 See Alfred C. Skaife, Early California Law Books (1847-1850), 1 SAN FRANCISCO BAR 12-16 (Feb. 1937); Early California Law Books (1850-51), 1 SFB 7-13 (June 1937); Early California Law Books (1852-53), 1 SFB 8-10 (Oct. 1937); Early California Law Books (1854), 1 SFB 5-7 (Dec. 1937); Early California Law Books (1855-56), 2 SFB 11-14 (April 1938); Early California Law Books (1857), 2 SFB 6-9 (Aug. 1938); Early California Law Books (1858), 3 SFB 14-16 (Feb. 1939); Early California Law Books, 5 SFB 12-14 (April 1941) and GORDON MORRIS BAKKEN, PRACTICING LAW IN FRONTIER CALIFORNIA (1991).

This short piece discusses book publisher H.H. Bancroft's efforts to resolve this supply issue by bringing practical and cost-effective law books to lawyers in antebellum California. By examining two of his company's catalogues, important insights can be gleaned not only about the legal information needs of early California lawyers, but also Bancroft's innovative agency business model which linked both sides of the United States continent through the antebellum legal publishing industry.[2]

Hubert Howe Bancroft was born on May 5, 1832, in Granville, Ohio.[3] As a teenager he thought of becoming a lawyer, but the fortuitous marriage of his sister into the Derby bookselling family led him to decide that the book trade was his destiny.[4] At age sixteen he moved to Buffalo, N.Y. to clerk in his brother-in-law's bookshop, George H. Derby & Co. This was not a happy arrangement. Bancroft was relegated to doing minor tasks, which led to tension with Derby. Bancroft's discontent with his lowly status at his brother-in-law's bookstore led him to return to Ohio. Derby, however, did not abandon the young man and gave him several cases of books to sell back in Ohio.[5] Bancroft acquired a horse and cart, became an itinerant bookseller and found that he was quite successful in this endeavor. This success, the news of the fortunes being made, and the large increases in

---

2 In her 1931 study on the book publishing industry in San Francisco, University of California librarianship student Ruth Doxsee dedicated a section to the history of the Bancroft publishing company. While Doxsee's work is a straight-forward and factual account of Bancroft, there is no detailed discussion of his law book catalogs or the innovative agency business model he built. Ruth Doxsee, Book Publishing in San Francisco (1848 to 1906) (May 1931) (Special Study, University of California School of Librarianship) (on file with the University of California-Berkeley).

3 JOHN WALTON CAUGHEY, HUBERT HOWE BANCROFT: HISTORIAN OF THE WEST 6 (1946).

4 *Id.* at 12-13.

5 *Id.* at 14.

[*Portrait of Hubert Howe Bancroft, standing holding top hat and cane*].

Image courtesy of California Faces: Selections from The Bancroft Library
Portrait Collection, The Bancroft Library, University of California, Berkeley.

population and wealth in California led his brother-in-law to send Bancroft out to the West Coast in 1852 with $5,000 worth of books to sell.[6]

The trip to California was not easy—Bancroft embarked from New York and spent five weeks on a series of Panama steamers before he reached San Francisco—but the voyage proved to be a success. Bancroft returned to the East and developed a plan to move out to San Francisco permanently and open a full-service bookstore. He obtained $10,000 in credit and hired his former fellow clerk at Derby's bookstore, George L. Kenny, to work with him.[7] And so, in 1856, the H.H. Bancroft and Company publishing and bookselling empire began and with it, the major source for law books, both published elsewhere and published in California. Fortunately, copies of Bancroft's first two catalogues, the 1857 and 1858 catalogues, still exist, and provide a remarkable window into law practice in California during the period immediately before the Civil War.

The legal education of lawyers in early California depended, in part, on the availability of law books, as did the practice of law throughout the nineteenth century.[8] In preparation for the bar, aspiring attorneys studied Blackstone, Story, Kent, and other influential jurists of the time. Even seasoned members of the California bar were reliant on the availability of law books to keep current on their knowledge of the law. Those treatises depended upon by California's bar included Blackstone's *Commentaries*, Zephaniah Swift's *Digest of the Law of Evidence*, Simon Greenleaf's *Evidence*, Joseph Story's *Commentaries*, and Jame's Kent's *Commentaries on American Law*.[9]

The greatest problem for California attorneys in the 1850s, however, was obtaining law books. While preparing for a case in

---

6 *Id.* at 17.

7 *Id.*

8 Bakken, *supra* note 1, at 26.

9 *Id.* at 27.

July 1856, Attorney Charles Huse of Santa Barbara mused in his journal, "The more I examine it, the more difficulties I find, and I regret that I do not have the books of authorities to satisfactorily resolve the many questions which are presented."[10] Fortunately, a lawyer friend loaned Huse the necessary books. Correspondence between lawyers during this time demonstrates a system of unofficial libraries whereby books were passed from one person to another, further illustrating the lack of access to legal information in early California.[11]

Likewise, a law bookseller in antebellum California faced a number of difficulties. The first and most important was acquiring books to sell. A few California statutes and government documents were printed locally in small quantities, but the majority of working books that a lawyer would have needed could not have been locally sourced. Instead, they needed to come from the law publishing centers on the East Coast. The Overland Trail was dangerous and unpredictable and slow. Before the establishment of the transcontinental railroad, the better route was the one Bancroft took to California from New York.[12]

As the United States Post Office Department observed in June 1850, "The extraordinary migration caused by the discoveries of gold in California, and the wonderful growth of settlement and business in that region, have occasioned the placing [of] a large and increasing number of steamships and other vessels on this route, on both oceans."[13] But this was by no means an easy or inexpensive way to transport goods, including books. The route involved changing ships, which meant during the process of transferring cargo, books could be lost or damaged. The ships

---

10 *Id.* at 29.

11 *Id.* at 27.

12 *See* CAUGHEY, *supra* note 3, at 18-29.

13 LETTER FROM THE POSTMASTER GENERAL TRANSMITTING INFORMATION IN RELATION TO CONTRACTS FOR THE TRANSPORTATION OF THE MAILS BETWEEN NEW YORK AND CALIFORNIA, H.R. Doc. No. 32-124, 36 (1852).

and the warehouses enroute were always at risk of fire. Agents in the various ports might pilfer cargo. And, of course, ships could be lost. If all went well, the route could still take five weeks or more. Bancroft stocked his new business with books that took the sea route around Cape Horn. He was lucky; the books arrived undamaged.[14]

As noted above, California was growing exponentially during the first half of the 1850s, and a system for delivering the mail between New York and California was in proportion to the increased demand for means of transportation, to which there seemed to be no limit. New routes were being opened across the continent. In addition to the Isthmus of Panama route, there was another via San Juan de Nicaragua and a third, the "Tehuantepec" route. However, the Postmaster General, in a letter to Congress in 1852, reported:

> I have the honor to state, that there is not in the possession of this department any official or other reliable information establishing the fact that there is now in successful operation any ocean route between New York and San Francisco affording opportunity for the transportation of the United States mail between those points with greater economy and dispatch (sic) than is now afforded by the way of Chagres and Panama.[15]

---

14 By Congressional action on March 3, 1847, the first contracts were made for the transportation of mail between New York and San Francisco via the Panama Isthmus. These 10-year contracts called for the commissioning of eight steamships "sheathed with copper...fitted with iron side-wheels, with good and sufficient boilers...and to be so placed below the water-line as to be as far as practicable beyond the reach of cannon-shot." By 1852, there were six existing contracts for the transportation of mail between New York and San Francisco, and according to a July 21, 1852 letter from the Postmaster General to the House of Representatives, three offers for additional mail transportation by steamship companies were placed before the Postmaster Department. LETTER FROM THE POSTMASTER GENERAL, *supra* note 2, at 2-6.

15 *Id.* at 2, 13.

This delivery system was an important ingredient to Bancroft's future success as a law bookseller. As an example, in August of 1852 alone, 85,000 letters were carried to and from the Atlantic coast to California.[16]

Law booksellers sold more than just law books, as the discussion of the 1857 catalogue will reveal. Law booksellers throughout the U.S. not only sold law books, but, also, blank books, paper, pens, and other articles necessary to carry in the practice of law.[17] The conventional wisdom was that a successful law bookseller needed to provide a "one stop" shop for his lawyer customers. Bancroft understood this. And, therefore, his shop offered a wide range of goods for his lawyer customers. Bancroft also realized that selling law books alone was probably a road to financial disaster. So, his shop, from its beginning, also offered other types of books, especially schoolbooks which were always in high demand, and thus sold very well.

THE 1857 CATALOGUE

In 1857, Bancroft published a comprehensive catalogue of his stock for sale offering law, school, and medical books as well as an assortment of other stationery and office supplies.[18]

In the short introduction to the catalogue Bancroft made an interesting claim: "we will sell the best articles in our line at lower rates than ever before offered in California."[19] This was actually a rather extraordinary claim. Perhaps it was simply puffery, but if Bancroft was able to offer his merchandise at lower prices than his competitors, then he either had been able to negotiate lower costs for the items or lower transportation costs. Eastern booksellers routinely gave a discount to resellers who bought in bulk. It is possible that Bancroft was able to negotiate a larger discount by buying larger

---

16 *Id.* at 29.

17 M.H. HOEFLICH, LEGAL PUBLISHING IN ANTEBELLUM AMERICA 68 (2010).

18 H.H. BANCROFT, CATALOGUE OF H.H. BANCROFT & CO (1857).

19 *Id.* at 3.

CATALOGUE

OF

H. H. BANCROFT & CO.

BOOKSELLERS,

Publishers and Stationers,

IMPORTERS OF

LAW, SCHOOL, MEDICAL,

MISCELLANEOUS, BLANK BOOKS,

AND

STATIONERY,

MONTGOMERY STREET,

SAN FRANCISCO.

quantities. At any rate, the offer of high quality at lower cost certainly would have been attractive to potential customers.

The substantive part of the catalogue begins with a list of books that Bancroft claimed to publish himself. These were primarily schoolbooks, although two might have appealed to lawyers, *The Revised Clerks' Assistant for California* and *The American Almanac for 1857.*[20] Both of these books were variants of books published in other locales in the United States but edited and supplemented to have useful information specifically for California residents. This type of localized publishing was common throughout the United States and Bancroft realized that he could serve his customers by providing these types of publications and build his customer base thereby.

The catalogue offers a wide selection of stationery available for purchase, featuring "Kent Mills Writing Papers" which are touted to be "suitable for the American market." There are two possible ways to interpret the phrase "suitable for the American market." The first is that the papers were imported from England and the name may refer to a series of paper mills that were in operation in the County of Kent and collectively referred to as the Kent Mills.[21] The other possibility is that the papers came from a mill in New York which also operated under the name "Kent Mills."[22] Regardless of whether the papers were imported from England or New York, they were not locally made. This is further evidence of Bancroft's business acumen in importing necessary and practical items for California's legal community.

Also offered was stationery from other famous American and English paper manufacturers, such as De La Rue & Co., Rhoads & Sons, and Whatman's and Hollingsworth. These various manufacturers provided a large and diverse choice of writing

---

20 *Id.* at 4.

21 ALFRED H. SHORTER, STUDIES ON THE HISTORY OF PAPERMAKING IN BRITAIN 213 (1993)

22 Bancroft, *supra* note 17, at 5. *See generally* LYMAN H. WEEKS, A HISTORY OF PAPER-MANUFACTURING IN THE UNITED STATES, 1690-1916 (1916).

paper for every imaginable use, from ladies' social notes to commercial purposes. For the lawyer, there was King Mills legal cap as well as a wide range of so-called commercial and mercantile papers. There were also envelopes, including those manufactured for foreign postal systems.

The variety of stationery available from Bancroft for the general public as well as for lawyers is quite instructive. During the nineteenth century, there was what might almost be called a fetish about having a specific article for every writing task.[23] The best example of this is the number of pieces found in the typical upper class Victorian table place setting. In terms of stationery, a lawyer would have wanted high quality, rag or linen thick stationery for client correspondence, less expensive paper for writing briefs and other everyday documents, vellum, or at least extremely high-quality paper for wills and other documents that needed to be engrossed, and scrap paper for receipts or similar purposes.[24] In addition, a lawyer who used a copy press would need special paper or copy books for these purposes.

Indeed, Bancroft's store offered more than just books and stationery for lawyers. He offered seven different sizes of copying presses and all the accoutrements to operate them. Such presses were a critical time saving device for antebellum lawyers, since they eliminated the need for a scrivener to make multiple copies of documents such as letters. The shop also offered a variety of document and deed boxes. When Bancroft opened his shop, vertical files were still unknown, and lawyers had used document boxes in wood or tin for centuries as a primary means of document storage.[25]

---

23 J. WILLIS WESTLAKE, HOW TO WRITE LETTERS: A MANUAL OF CORRESPONDENCE, SHOWING THE CORRECT STRUCTURE, COMPOSITION, PUNCTUATION, FORMALITIES, AND USES OF THE VARIOUS KINDS OF LETTERS, NOTES, AND CARDS 15-19 (Philadelphia, Sower, Potts & Co. 1876).

24 *See generally* AJ Valente, *Changes in Print Paper During the 19th Century*, Proceedings of the Charleston Library Conference, 2010.

25 M.H. Hoeflich, *From Scriveners to Typewriters: Document Production in the*

Document production was a primary activity for lawyers, so in addition to the wide variety of papers Bancroft sold, he also sold pens, inks, pen stands and other writing items. One of the more interesting items offered were lawyers' seals. These were offered in two types: Vandyke edged and "checquered red (sic)"[26] in multiple sizes. And, of course, there was sealing wax available in 4, 8, 10, and 20 sticks to the pound.

By making all these items easily available to his customers at a reduced rate, Bancroft was able to serve all their legal writing needs. From stationery to writing instruments to file organization, Bancroft's was indeed a one stop shop for stocking a law office.

The list of law books available from Bancroft's store in 1857 was impressive. The preface to the list states:

LAW BOOKS,
AT GREATLY REDUCED PRICES.

We would call particular attention to our Stock of Law Books, by far the best in the country.

We have arrangements with all the leading Publishers, by which we purchase on *better terms than any House in the United States.*

We will make special terms with Lawyers, according to the Amount, making it for their interest to give us their orders in preference to New-York.[27]

There are several quite significant points in this brief preface. The most significant is what this tells us of Bancroft's business model in 1857. Effectively, Bancroft is presenting himself as a local agent for purchasers as an alternative to purchasing books by

---

Nineteenth-Century Law Office, 16 THE GREEN BAG 408 (2013).

26 BANCROFT, *supra* note 14, at 16.

27 *Id.* at 24.

mail. It is impossible to know how many books Bancroft actually had in stock in his California shop, but it seems rather likely that he did not stock even a majority of the books he lists as available for purchase (as will become apparent). Second, in 1857 Bancroft almost certainly had not established a special relationship with any Eastern booksellers or he would have stated this, as he does in his 1858 catalogue. Third, the 1857 list of books available is completely unpriced. This, combined with the language of the preface, indicates that prices would vary depending upon the actual cost to Bancroft.

This agency model that is reflected in the 1857 catalogue would have had several practical effects. First, the model involved the possibility of a substantial time period between the order and receipt of the book, especially if the purchaser wanted a set price in advance of committing to buy. On the other hand, the time and expense involved for the individual who chose to order personally rather than through an agent like Bancroft may well have been greater. More significant, perhaps, is whether the ordinary California lawyer would have regularly received Eastern law booksellers' and publishers' catalogues. We may speculate that some did, but that others did not. Bancroft would have had better knowledge of the list of lawyers in California than Eastern booksellers.

Another significant advantage for individual book purchasers in California of purchasing books from Bancroft rather than Eastern booksellers was the problem of payment. Before 1863 there was no national paper currency. Local business transactions were carried on in locally issued bank currency.[28] The value of this locally issued currency was stabilized and maintained by the issuing banks. The value of the currency outside the area in which it had been issued fluctuated, and indeed, currency issued by a particular bank in California might not be accepted by a Boston

---

28 George A. Selgin and Lawrence H. White, *Monetary Reform and the Redemption of National Bank Notes, 1863-1913*, 68 THE BUSINESS HIST. REV. 206 (1994).

or New York bank at all. This necessitated using bills of exchange and other means of money transfer.[29] For a business like Bancroft's, such out of state transactions were common and followed established patterns. For an individual lawyer who wanted a few books, this would have been a serious burden. Buying through Bancroft rather than directly from Eastern booksellers made this process far simpler.

The 1857 catalogue contains ten pages of law book listings. Included are all the U.S. Supreme Court Reports beginning in 1790 and a selection of U.S. Circuit Court Reports from 1810 through 1854, as well as the U.S. Statutes at Large, several digests of federal opinions, and state reports from California, Indiana, Kentucky, Louisiana, Massachusetts, Missouri, New York, and Ohio. There is a small selection of the English reports, viz. English Common Law Reports, East's King's Bench Reports, English Exchequer Reports, and English Chancery Reports. The small number of English reports listed for sale may indicate Bancroft's judgment that a greater number of English reports would be unlikely to sell or, more likely, that those listed were the ones that he believed he could most easily obtain for customers.

The remaining seven pages of law books that he listed for sale were treatises. Among these treatises, Bancroft listed most of the standard American and English treatises available from Eastern booksellers. He listed, among others, two editions of Blackstone, four of Chitty's treatises, Coke on Littleton, Greenleaf on Evidence, Hoffman's Legal Study, Kent's *Commentaries*, and ten volumes by Justice Story.

Among the civil law books, Bancroft listed Browne's treatise on civil and admiralty law, Cooper's *Justinian's Institutes*, Domat's treatise on civil law, and Pothier on Contracts. It is worth noting, however, that Bancroft's selection of civil law books was actually smaller than that available in most Eastern booksellers' catalogues, indicating that he did not make any effort to provide his customers with a large variety of civil law texts.

---

29 *Id.*

It is also interesting that the catalogue listed a number of works specifically for California lawyers and others that would have been of particular interest to California lawyers because of California's civil law heritage from Mexico. Bancroft offered two Mexican law guides in 1857: Rockwell's treatise on Mexican law and Schmidt's treatise on Mexican law. Once again, it is interesting to note that Bancroft did not offer a greater variety of treatises on Mexican or South American law, effectively limiting his offerings to English language texts.

Bancroft also offered two California specific texts which he published. The first was *The Revised Clerks' Assistant for California and Oregon*, a form book. The second was *The American Almanac... California Edition*. The form book was a basic collection of model documents and similar in format and content to other volumes of this sort available in virtually every American jurisdiction. The *Almanac* was aimed directly at lawyers but was a compendium of useful knowledge that lawyers would have valued. Neither book, however, was truly an original legal text. In addition, he offered the California reports and the California statutes. He also offered the *Lawyers and Justices California Form Book*.

THE 1858 CATALOGUE

The next law catalogue issued by Bancroft in 1858 reveals some significant changes to his business model as well as to the stock itself. First, the 1858 catalogue is devoted exclusively to law books and the front cover reveals the specific details of Bancroft's agency arrangements (including non-law books).[30]

The preface to the actual list of law books reads:

> H.H.B. & Co., are the sole Agents for the sale of Messrs. LITTLE BROWN & COMPANY'S Publications, and being also in direct communication, under new arrangements, with

---

30 H.H. BANCROFT, H.H. BANCROFT & CO.'S LAW CATALOGUE (1858).

H. H. BANCROFT & CO'S
LAW CATALOGUE.

Messrs Little, Brown & Co's Miscellaneous Books.

Over 10,000 Volumes Messrs. Harper's publications, at an addition of actual expense only, to the publishers prices. For New Books, see last number Harper's Magazine.

Agents for the sale of Messrs. Derby & Jackson's publications, of which we keep in store, a stock of about 12,000 Volumes.

From New York, Boston and Philadelphia, we are in constant receipt of the choicest works in every department of English and American Literature.

A Fair Assortment Medical Books.

Sole Agents for the Standard Series of School Books, by far the best and most attractive ever before used in Schools.

Messrs. J. G. Shaw & Co's Blank Work only.

A very heavy Stock at all times, of from the cheapest American to the finest English STATIONERY, at a still further reduction in prices.

The attention of the trade is respectfully called to our fine assortment of goods and our superior facilities.

all the Law Book Publishers, they sell, with but few exceptions, in quantities or by the single volume, at the Eastern Catalogue Prices, thus giving their customers the direct benefit of every advantage they possess in the way of buying, and reserving only for themselves cost and a small commission.[31]

This refined business model was brilliant. First, Bancroft had concluded an agreement with Little, Brown to be their *exclusive* agent for law books. Of course, this statement does not state whether Bancroft had sole rights throughout California or limited to Northern California and San Francisco, but even if these rights were limited to San Francisco, they would have been of great value. Second, the preface states that Bancroft had made new arrangements with all other law book publishers and was in "direct communication" with them to obtain books. At the least, this suggests to the customer that Bancroft could obtain these books more quickly than other sellers.

When one thinks about these agency arrangements created by Bancroft, one begins to recognize that he set up a law bookselling business model which relieved him of the need to maintain a large stock of expensive law books and, at the same time, required customers to patronize his business if they wanted to obtain locally produced books from Little, Brown, then the largest law bookseller in the United States. From the perspective of the customer, he paid the same as he would have done had he ordered directly from Little, Brown's catalogue. From Bancroft's perspective, he covered his costs and received a commission. Since most Eastern booksellers routinely gave out-of-state booksellers a substantial discount, the commissions that Bancroft received (i.e., his profit) may even have been a bit more than "a small commission."

---

31 *Id.* at 2.

When H.H. Bancroft established his bookstore and publishing company in 1857, he created a business model that worked for a burgeoning city and region that was far distant from the primary sources of books on the East Coast of the United States. Through this innovative agency business model as applied to publishing, Bancroft was able to offer law books and document production articles necessary for the practice of law, at a reduced price, for members of the California legal community. The model's success is witnessed by the continuation of the business for over a century and a half and made Bancroft & Company one of the most influential law booksellers in the United States.

In 1869, at the same time the "Golden Spike" was being driven at Promontory Point, Utah, Bancroft built one of the largest buildings in San Francisco to house his business. Six months later, the last leg of the Transcontinental Railroad from Sacramento to San Francisco Bay was completed. Bancroft became the largest publishing house west of Chicago, when in 1886 he merged with Sumner Whitney, another law book publisher in San Francisco, to create the Bancroft-Whitney Company. Sadly, the entire plant was destroyed by the Great Fire and Earthquake of 1906, but in 1910, thanks to financial aid from his attorney customer base, Bancroft-Whitney reopened for business. For the next 80 years, the company continued to meet the information needs of the legal profession, producing such publications as *California Jurisprudence*, *Texas Jurisprudence*, *Florida Jurisprudence*, and *American Law Reports* (published jointly with The Lawyers Co-operative Publishing Company).[32] In 1989, International Thomson acquired both Lawyers Co-operative and Bancroft-Whitney in a $810 million dollar bidding contest.[33] If only Bancroft himself could have seen how far his law book shop had come.

---

32 W.E. Kuhl, *Bancroft-Whitney Company Celebrates Its Centennial Year*, 61 CASE & COM 3-10 (1956).

33 Nancy H. Kreisler, *Thomson in Deal for Lawyers Co-op*, N.Y. TIMES, May 3, 1989, at 105.

9 781616 196967